ONE HUNDRED GREAT BOOKS IN HAIKU

David Bader

VIKING
an imprint of
PENGUIN BOOKS

VIKING

Published by the Penguin Group
Penguin Books Ltd, 80 Strand, London WC2R ORL, England
Penguin Group (USA) Inc., 375 Hudson Street, New York, New York 10014, USA
Penguin Group (Canada), 90 Eglinton Avenue East, Suite 700,
Toronto, Ontario, Canada M4P 2Y3
(a division of Pearson Penguin Canada Inc.)
Penguin Ireland, 25 St Stephen's Green, Dublin 2, Ireland
(a division of Penguin Books Ltd)
Penguin Group (Australia), 250 Camberwell Road,
Camberwell, Victoria 3124, Australia (a division of Pearson Australia Group Pty Ltd)
Penguin Books India Pvt Ltd, 11 Community Centre,
Panchsheel Park, New Delhi – 110 017, India
Penguin Group (NZ), cnr Airborne and Rosedale Roads, Albany,
Auckland 1310, New Zealand (a division of Pearson New Zealand Ltd)
Penguin Books (South Africa) (Pty) Ltd, 24 Sturdee Avenue,
Rosebank 2196, South Africa

Penguin Books Ltd, Registered Offices: 80 Strand, London WC2R ORL, England

www.penguin.com

First published 2005
1

Set in 11.25/13pt Adobe Garamond
Typeset by Rowland Phototypesetting Ltd, Bury St Edmunds, Suffolk
Printed in Great Britain by Clays Ltd, St Ives plc

A CIP catalogue record for this book is available from the British Library

ISBN-13: 978-0-670-91577-4
ISBN-10: 0-670-91577-7

ONE HUNDRED
GREAT BOOKS
IN HAIKU

Acknowledgements

The author thanks the many people who helped him condense, edit and trample the great books into seventeen syllables: editors Zelda Turner and Erin Moore; literary agents John Boswell, Lauren Galit and Christa Bourg; Valerie Stanford; and bibliophile and attorney-at-law Benjamin E. Rosenberg Esq., who generously contributed many useful suggestions without even billing for his time. The author also thanks his parents, whose love and encouragement over the years helped him become educated way beyond his intelligence. Most of all, the author acknowledges his debt to the towering writers and thinkers who inspired this book. He takes full blame for all mistakes, except when it is obviously their fault.

Foreword

In the fifteenth century, Gutenberg's movable-type printing press revolutionized the world of publishing. Previously, books had been so scarce that it was not uncommon for a library to have only a handful of bound Latin manuscripts, chained to a desk. Beach reading was rare and required furniture movers. After Gutenberg, millions of books on all subjects were published, some of them highly influential, 'great', or at least very long. This in turn led to eyestrain, paper cuts, deforestation and adult reading groups.

In Japan, meanwhile, the seventeen-syllable haiku began to emerge. Developed by Zen monks possibly suffering from attention deficit disorder, these poems were packed with keen insights on frogs and cherry blossom yet short enough to be recited in a single breath. Japanese readers could experience and savour the finest haiku of Bashō in its entirety (three lines), while Western readers of, say, John Milton's *Paradise Lost* (10,000 lines) were still staring at the title page.

This collection attempts to combine these two breakthroughs. Condensed into haiku, the 'Great Books' are now within reach of even the shortest attention spans. The formal requirements of haiku (three lines of five, seven and five syllables, respectively) have, admittedly, made it necessary to cut some things, such as characters, plot, dialogue and descriptive passages. Still, these are small sacrifices in view of the huge savings in time and shelf space. As an added benefit, when asked, 'Did you really get all the way through *War and Peace*?' readers can now suavely reply, 'No, but I read the haiku.'

Deciding which books to include was difficult, as there were so many worthy candidates. In the end, selections were made on the basis of a scientific formula that took into consideration historical importance, originality, weight (in hardcover) and impact on the reader (both as a book and as a sedative). The result is this set of one hundred haiku, designed to be read and enjoyed without interfering with anyone's weekend plans. At the end, there will not be a quiz.

THE CANTERBURY TALES
Geoffrey Chaucer

Pilgrimmes on spryng braecke –
roadde trippe! Whoe farrtted? Yiuw didde.
Noe, naught meae. Yaes, yiuw.

THE ILIAD

Homer

Sing, Goddess, of how
brooding Achilles' mood swings
caused him to act out.

OEDIPUS REX

Sophocles

Chorus: Poor bastard.
Oedipus: This is awful!
Blind Seer: Told you so.

REMEMBRANCE OF
THINGS PAST

Marcel Proust

Tea-soaked madeleine –
a childhood recalled. I had
brownies like that once.

PHAEDO
Plato

By Zeus, Socrates!
It seems you're right once again!
Time for your hemlock.

THE ODYSSEY
Homer

Aegean forecast –
storms, chance of one-eyed giants,
delays expected.

DE REVOLUTIONIBUS
ORBIUM CAELESTIUM
Nicolaus Copernicus

Guessus whatibus?
Earthus orbits the Sunnum!
Ptolemy doofus.

BEOWULF

Hrothgar's hall,   haunted.
Dauntless Danes die,   Grendel-gored.
Why not   hrelocate?

MEDITATIONS
Marcus Aurelius

As grapes become wine,
so must one accept one's fate.
Die well. Like a grape.

THE INFERNO

Dante Alighieri

Abandon all hope!
Looks like everyone's down here.
Omigod – the Pope!

MOBY-DICK

Herman Melville

Vengeance! Black blood! Aye!
Doubloons to him that harpoons
the Greenpeace dinghy.

THE CONFESSIONS

St Augustine

This is just to say
I screwed around. Forgive me.
I enjoyed it so.

PRIDE AND PREJUDICE
Jane Austen

Single white lass seeks
landed gent for marriage, whist.
No parsons, thank you.

BLEAK HOUSE
Charles Dickens

Fog, gloom, men in wigs –
the Chancery Court blights all.
See where law school leads?

THE PRINCE

Niccolò Machiavelli

What I learned at court:
Being more feared than loved – good.
Getting poisoned – bad.

DISCOURSE ON METHOD

René Descartes

If I think, I am.
If I don't exist, how do
I know about me?

CLARISSA, OR, THE HISTORY
OF A YOUNG LADY:
COMPREHENDING THE MOST
IMPORTANT CONCERNS OF
PRIVATE LIFE AND
PARTICULARLY SHOWING THE
DISTRESSES THAT MAY ATTEND
THE MISCONDUCT BOTH OF
PARENTS AND CHILDREN, IN
RELATION TO MARRIAGE

Samuel Richardson

To Miss Howe: Send help!
I've been raped in Volume Six
with three more to go.

THE EPIC OF GILGAMESH

Part god, part mortal,
offspring of a mixed marriage.
King Gilgamesh copes.

AS I LAY DYING

William Faulkner

Addie: I'm dyin'.
Darl: I'm nuts. Mules: We're drownded.
Anse: Need me some teeth.

ROBINSON CRUSOE
Daniel Defoe

Alone for twelve years,
then a footprint in the sand.
Thank God! A servant!

MADAME BOVARY
Gustave Flaubert

Poor foolish Emma,
ruined by romance novels.
Could haiku have helped?

THE WEALTH OF NATIONS

Adam Smith

Supply meets demand.
The invisible hand claps.
Capitalist Zen.

DAS KAPITAL

Karl Marx

October winds blow.
Your contradictions doom you,
capitalist swine.

THE HISTORIES

Herodotus

Go tell the Spartans –
the Persian hordes are fierce and
wear funny slippers.

GULLIVER'S TRAVELS
Jonathan Swift

Thus I was first great,
then small, and much vexed to learn
that size *does* matter.

LITTLE WOMEN
Louisa May Alcott

Snowdrops hang like tears.
Shy, sweet, saintly Beth has died.
One down, three to go.

LORD OF THE FLIES
William Golding

'Kill him! Spill his blood!'
Marooned lads hold savage rites.
Choirboys learn to prey.

THE COUNT OF MONTE CRISTO
Alexandre Dumas

Gallant avenger.
Egg-dipped cheese sandwich. Thy name
is Monte Cristo.

WAITING FOR GODOT

Samuel Beckett

Act I. 'It's hopeless.
My boots don't fit. Where is God?'
Act II. The same thing.

BRIDESHEAD REVISITED

Evelyn Waugh

Gay Catholic toffs –
what else to expect from a
man named Evelyn?

DON QUIXOTE

Miguel de Cervantes

Dusk – the windmills turn.
Is the Don mad, or are we?
No, it's him all right.

HAMLET
William Shakespeare

'His mother wed his
dead murdered father's brother!'
Next Jerry Springer.

THE SCARLET LETTER
Nathaniel Hawthorne

Grim, grey New England –
all adulterers receive
free monogramming.

METAPHYSICS
Aristotle

Substance has essence.
Form adds whatness to thatness.
Whatsits have thinghood.

CANDIDE, OR, OPTIMISM
Voltaire

A naive young man
learns that bad things do happen
to smug *philosophes*.

WUTHERING HEIGHTS

Emily Brontë

Wild. Strange. A bit damp.
Heathcliff waits for Cathy's ghost.
Women. Always late.

PHILOSOPHIAE NATURALIS PRINCIPIA MATHEMATICA

Isaac Newton

Cherry blossoms fall
with Force equal to Mass times
Acceleration.

LADY CHATTERLEY'S LOVER

D. H. Lawrence

On the grounds, fresh game.
On the new gamekeeper, fresh
Lady Chatterley.

THE JUNGLE
Upton Sinclair

Slaughterhouse karma –
the dying ox returns as
Durham's Potted Meat.

THE HISTORY OF THE
DECLINE AND FALL OF
THE ROMAN EMPIRE

Edward Gibbon

From[1] rule[2] to[3] ruin.[4]
Rome's[5] last[6] words[7]: 'Help! I've fallen
and I can't get up.'[8]

---

[1] Tertullian, *Apol.*, c. 6, p. 80.

[2] In the Second Century of the Christian Era, this ancient and renowned power, the *Imperium Romanum, amplitudo quae fuit Roma* – you know, Rome – held dominion over lands spanning three continents, from oceanfront property in Spain to valuable time-shares in the Euphrates valley, its gentle yet powerful influence comprehending the most civilized portion of mankind and most of the best restaurants.

[3] Pliny the Elder, *Hist. Natur.*, l. vi. c. 32. Also Pliny the Younger, *Letters*, vi, xiv. In fact, the whole Pliny family agrees on this.

[4] For such was its state when Rome, suffering from its own immoderate greatness, its aims achieved by conquest undone by misrule, its martial spirit enfeebled by religion, its defences breached by barbarism, its head throbbing and its tongue fuzzy from a major post-orgy hangover, moaned, staggered a few steps, and just keeled over. For more on the orgies, see Lacivius, *De Perversitate* (Leyden ed.).

[5] See fn. 2, *supra*. Seven hills, all roads lead to it, gladiators. Enough said.

[6] The sedulous reader, feeling the exasperation of a long journey whose destination seems ever out of reach, anticipating that the attainment of the goal may require some fortifying infusion, following the example of the author who, himself, has needed a bracing libation on not a few occasions, particularly during his digression on Bulgarian armaments, may here find it salutary to avail himself of the revivifying powers of spirits, perhaps a double.

[7] For a few words on the decline of the Eastern Empire and the career of Mahomet, including his summer jobs, see Volumes V–VI.

[8] *'Succurre! Cecidi nec surgere possum.'*

OLD GORIOT

Honoré de Balzac

His two spoiled daughters –
they don't write, they don't visit.
This is gratitude?

CRIME AND PUNISHMENT

Fyodor Dostoyevsky

I, Rodya, killed her
to prove my theory. Uh oh.
Back to square oneski.

THE LIFE AND OPINIONS OF TRISTRAM SHANDY, GENTLEMAN

Laurence Sterne

I've torn out line two.

Reader, it was dull.

LOLITA

Vladimir Nabokov

Lecherous linguist –
he lays low and is laid low
after laying Lo.

THE CRITIQUE OF PURE REASON

Immanuel Kant

We are born knowing
circles to be circular.
We just don't know it.

THE CHERRY ORCHARD

Anton Chekhov

Their bankrupt estate
sold to a former servant.
Nobles down, serfs up.

DISCIPLINE AND PUNISH: THE BIRTH OF THE PRISON

Michel Foucault

Carceral discourse
polyvalently deployed.
Hot air gently blows.

REFLECTIONS ON THE
REVOLUTION IN FRANCE

Edmund Burke

Rights of man? Humbug!
And ladies? I pine for you,
Marie Antoinette.

FRANKENSTEIN

Mary Shelley

A mad scientist
creates a ghastly Monster
who just wants a hug.

THE METAMORPHOSIS
Franz Kafka

'What have I become?'
Uncertain, Gregor Samsa
puts out some feelers.

1 9 8 4

George Orwell

Love is a thoughtcrime.
The Thought Police make Winston
forget whatsername.

PHENOMENOLOGY OF SPIRIT

Georg Wilhelm Friedrich Hegel

Thesis: A whole pig.
Antithesis: Butcher shop.
Synthesis: Schnitzel.

THE TALE OF GENJI
Lady Murasaki Shikibu

Two wives, ten consorts –
under the wisteria,
many warm futons.

THE LIFE OF
SAMUEL JOHNSON
James Boswell

That night, as we supped,
he roared, 'Pass the salt, blockhead.'
The great man liked me.

JANE EYRE

Charlotte Brontë

O woe! His mad wife –
in the attic! Had they but
lived together first.

DOCTOR FAUSTUS
Christopher Marlowe

A scholar trades a
few fun years for endless Hell.
Maths was not his field.

TWO TREATISES OF GOVERNMENT
John Locke

Orange butterfly,
you have no divine right to
be called the 'monarch'.

ONE HUNDRED YEARS
OF SOLITUDE
Gabriel García Márquez

Plagues, incest, madness,
human pig-children. *Dios!*
Where does the time go?

TARTUFFE, OR, THE IMPOSTOR

Molière

They try to outwit
a self-righteous hypocrite –
the first sitcom writ.

AN ESSAY ON THE PRINCIPLE OF POPULATION

Thomas Malthus

People multiply,
food does not. The good news is
there are wars and plagues.

WAR AND PEACE
Leo Tolstoy

Guns roar, Russia burns.
Where's Andrey? Who is Petya?
Confused, France retreats.

TO THE LIGHTHOUSE
Virginia Woolf

Boy, death, art, earwig –
summer at the beach recalled,
minus some details.

BEING AND NOTHINGNESS

Jean-Paul Sartre

Gentle Left Bank sun –
bluebirds chirp their empty songs.
We are all condemned.

IVANHOE

Sir Walter Scott

'Who dat fine knight be?'
asked the saucy Moorish wench.
'Dat be Ivan, ho.'

THE MAYOR OF
CASTERBRIDGE
Thomas Hardy

Undone by his past –
he once sold his wife and child.
Nobody's perfect.

TAO TE CHING
Lao Tzu

The eternal Tao.
To know it is not to know.
What is it? Don't ask.

ULYSSES

James Joyce

Like the cicada,
Molly takes many years to
say 'Yes' to Leo.

RELATIVITY: THE SPECIAL AND GENERAL THEORY

Albert Einstein

Cherry blossoms fall
at light speed through curved space-time
and land with a thud.

THE MAGIC MOUNTAIN

Thomas Mann

The TB 'rest cure'.
Haus Berghof. Death, Eros, and
all meals included.

KAMA SUTRA

Vatsayana

Advice for those in
a difficult position.
First, be flexible.

WALDEN, OR, LIFE IN THE WOODS
Henry David Thoreau

Morning: Pond-gazing.
Afternoon: Berry-picking.
What a hectic day.

SAINT JOAN
George Bernard Shaw

Strange girl. Hears voices.
But, by Jove, even in death
she lights up a room.

THE IMPORTANCE OF
BEING EARNEST

Oscar Wilde

Earnestly posing
as Ernest, Jack learns he's named
Ernest in earnest.

SIDDHARTHA

Hermann Hesse

The cycle of life –
as with spicy vindaloo,
all things return. *Om.*

THE CATCHER IN
THE RYE

J. D. Salinger

I flunked out again.
Crumby prep schools. Bunch of dopes.
Boy, I'm not kidding.

THE ORIGIN OF SPECIES

Charles Darwin

Galápagos finch –
the same beak as Aunt Enid's!
A theory is born.

THE GREAT GATSBY
F. Scott Fitzgerald

Beauty to weep for –
coral, azure, apple green.
His custom-made shirts.

THE SOCIAL CONTRACT

Jean-Jacques Rousseau

All vote. All consent.
It's like a big family.
Not mine, but someone's.

FATHERS AND SONS
Ivan Turgenev

A nihilist dies
without having achieved much.
Mission accomplished.

NANA
Émile Zola

Paris courtesan –
in her salon, men admire
her French Empire chest.

ALSO SPRACH ZARATHUSTRA
Friedrich Wilhelm Nietzsche

Kindness is weakness!
Abhor pity, worship strength!
Be an *über*-jerk!

FINNEGANS WAKE

James Joyce

Riverrun on and
by Jaisus s'dense! Bien alors,
scribbledehobble.

VANITY FAIR: A NOVEL WITHOUT A HERO

William Makepeace Thackeray

No title, no wealth.
Still, Becky climbs in Mayfair.
But how? Lying helps.

PORTRAIT OF A LADY
Henry James

Will she inherit?
Which suitor will she marry?
When will tea be served?

THE VARIETIES OF
RELIGIOUS EXPERIENCE
William James

Let's be pragmatic.
Saints, monks, mystics – their faith works.
So what if they're nuts?

THE TIN DRUM

Günter Grass

A shrieking, drumming
dwarf winds up in a madhouse.
It's a long story.

THE WILD DUCK
Henrik Ibsen

She has shot the duck!
No, Hedvig has shot herself.
[*Offstage, relieved quacks.*]

UTOPIA
Thomas More

An austere commune –
'Utopia'. It's Greek for
'Nice, if you're a monk.'

PARADISE LOST

John Milton

O'er and o'er God warned,
'Eate not th'Apple!' Man dids't and
God ballistick went.

BRAVE NEW WORLD
Aldous Huxley

Euphoric drugs, sex,
cloning, the past forgotten.
So what else is new?

THE GRAPES OF WRATH
John Steinbeck

Okie exodus –
Ma Joad's fambly keeps movin'.
Where are the darned grapes?

FAUST

Johann Wolfgang von Goethe

He's damned – no, he's saved!
For German engineering,
another triumph.

HEART OF DARKNESS

Joseph Conrad

The darkness darkened.
Oh, the horror, the horror.
It was horrible.

THE INTERPRETATION
OF DREAMS
Sigmund Freud

Old pond. Frog jumps in.
Repressed sexual desire,
clearly Oedipal.

THE ARCHETYPES AND
THE COLLECTIVE
UNCONSCIOUS

Carl Gustav Jung

A patient says he
sees the phallus of the sun.
But then, who doesn't?

THE WASTELAND
T. S. Eliot

April, cruel month!
Zerstört. Θανατος. Shantih.
And May's no picnic.

ESSAYS

Michel de Montaigne

Genteel French musings –
life, death, odd smells, my moustache.
Today's topic: Thumbs.

THE CALL OF THE WILD

Jack London

Alaskan tundra –
a dog finds his inner wolf.
White snows turn yellow.

MIDDLEMARCH
George Eliot

Stifling social roles,
small-town gossip – beware the
eyes of Middlemarch.

THE SUN ALSO RISES
Ernest Hemingway

'Why can't we?' she said.
'War wound,' I said. 'Oy,' Cohn said.
Back to Harry's Bar.

Index